Little Princess Easy Bake Oven Recipes

Jane Romsey

Published by Fat Dog Publishing LLC in 2015

First edition; First printing
Illustrations and design © 2015 Maz Scales

http://fatdogpublishing.com

ISBN: 978-1-943828-09-8

This book belongs to

Table of Contents

Angel Cookies   33
Angels White Cake   12
Angels White Cake Mix   11
Baby Brownies   22
Baked Apple   57
Birthday Cake   13
Blueberry Danish   50
Breakfast Biscuits   51
Bunny's Carrot Cake   9
Butter Cookies   35
Butterscotch Candy   56
Butterscotch Chip Cookies 44
Cheese Biscuits 61
Cheese Omelette   64
Cheesy Quesadilla   62
Choc Chip Peanut Cookies 41
Chocolate Cake 5
Chocolate Cake Mix   4
Chocolate Chip Cookies   39
Chocolate Chip Cookies   40
Chocolate Frosting   24
Chocolate Frosting Mix   23
Coconut Cake   8
Cookie Mix   38
Crazy Cake   14
Cream Cheese Frosting   29
Cream Cheese Frosting Mix   28
Cream Frosting 31
Frosting Mix   30
Ginger Cookies 45
Gooey Caramel Layer Bars 48
Haystacks 55
Home Made Bisquick Mix   60

Home Made Colored Sugar 1
Honey Bunches Snack 49
I Love Pink Cake 3
Kool Aid Cake 17
Kool Aid Cake Mix 16
Layer Cookies 42
Lemon Cake Mix 6
Lil' Princess 6
Lil' Princess Lemon Cake 7
Oatmeal Fruit Bars 47
Oreo Mud Pies 43
Party Frosting 32
Peach Upside Down Cake 19
Peanut Butter 31
Peanut Butter Cake 10
Peanut Butter Cookies 36
Peanut Butter Cream 30
Peanut Butter Fudge 53
Pizza 63
Princess Sparkle Tea Cakes 21
Quick Cake 20
Raisin 39
Raisin Bread Pudding 58
Raisin Spice Cake 15
Rice Krispie Treats 37
Santa's Cookies 46
Scones 52
Snow Mounds 54
Sparkly Frosting 25
Super Fun M and M's Cake 18
Thumbprint Cookies 34
Twisty Cheese Straws 59
White Frosting 27
White Frosting Mix 26
Yellow Cake Mix 2

Home Made Colored Sugar

2 tablespoons Sugar
2 to 3 drops food coloring (for vibrant colors)
1 drop food coloring (for softer colors)

Place sugar in a snack size ziplock bag.

Add food coloring of your choice and close securely.

Carefully use your fingers to spread the food coloring throughout the sugar and shake until desired color is achieved.

To make a very light pastel color, either use more sugar to a regular drop of coloring or a very, very tiny drop to the 2 tablespoons.

Store excess in the ziplock bag.

Yellow Cake Mix

6 teaspoons Flour
4 teaspoons Sugar
¼ teaspoon Baking Powder
Dash Salt
¼ teaspoon Vanilla Powder
2 teaspoons Shortening

Combine all ingredients, mixing well.
Place in a ziploc bag, seal until needed.

Makes 1 package Yellow Cake Mix.

To Use:
6 teaspoons milk
1 Package Mix

Grease and flour two Easy-Bake Oven pans.
Mix 1 package mix and milk.
Stir until batter is smooth.
Pour into prepared pans.
Bake in for 12 to 15 minutes or until sides separate from pan.

Remove and cool. Frost and serve.

2

I Love Pink Cake

5 tablespoons Flour
¼ teaspoon Baking Powder
⅛ teaspoon Salt
5 teaspoons Red Sugar Crystals
¼ teaspoon Vanilla
4 teaspoons Vegetable Oil
8 teaspoons Milk

Stir together cake flour, baking powder, salt,
red sugar, vanilla, oil and milk until the batter is
smooth and pink.

Pour 3 tablespoons of batter into greased and floured
cake pan.

Bake 15 minutes.

Repeat for second layer.

Makes 2 layers.

Chocolate Cake Mix

1 cup sugar

3 tablespoons unsweetened Cocoa Powder

1½ cups all purpose Flour

1 teaspoon Baking Soda

½ teaspoon Salt

⅓ cup Vegetable Shortening

In a medium bowl, combine sugar, cocoa powder, flour, baking soda, and salt.

Stir with a wire whisk until blended.

With a pastry blender, cut in shortening until mixture looks like fine breadcrumbs.

Spoon about ⅓ cup of the mixture into each of 11 small containers with tight fitting lids or zip lock bags.

Seal containers and label with date and contents.
Store in a cool dry place.

Use within 12 weeks. Makes 11 servings.

Chocolate Cake

To one container of chocolate cake mix (page 4) add 4 teaspoons water.

Stir with a fork or spoon until blended and smooth.

Pour mixture into greased and floured 4 inch round miniature baking pan.

Follow directions for child's oven or bake in mom's preheated 375 degree oven for 12 to 13 minutes.

Remove from oven and cool in pan on a rack for 5 minutes.

Invert onto a small plate and remove pan.

When cool frost with Children's Chocolate Frosting if desired.

Serves 2 children.

Lil' Princess
Lemon Cake Mix

1 cup sugar
1½ cups flour
1 teaspoon baking soda
½ teaspoon salt
1 teaspoon lemon Kool-Aid
⅓ cup vegetable shortening

Combine dry ingredients. Cut in shortening.

Spoon about ⅓ cup of the mixture into each of 11 small containers with tight fitting lids, or zip lock bags.

Seal containers and label with date and contents. Store in a cool dry place. Use within 12 weeks.

Makes 11 servings.

Lil' Princess Lemon Cake

Mix 1 package of Lil' Princess Lemon Cake Mix (page 6) with 1 tablespoon of water.

Stir well until smooth.

Bake in greased pan in oven until slightly brown.

Coconut Cake

1 package Yellow Cake Mix (page 2)
2 tablespoons Milk
3 tablespoons Coconut Cream Pudding Mix
1 teaspoon Shredded Coconut

Grease and flour two Easy Bake Oven pans.

Combine all the ingredients in small bowl, except the coconut, and mix until smooth.

Pour into prepared pans, sprinkle coconut on top.

Bake for 12 to 15 minutes or until sides separate from pan.

Remove and cool.

Bunny's Carrot Cake

2 packages Yellow Cake Mix (page 2)
⅛ teaspoon Ground Cinnamon
2 pinches Ground Nutmeg
2 pinches Ground Ginger
1 tablespoon grated Carrots
2 teaspoons canned crushed Pineapple
1 teaspoon beaten Egg
2½ teaspoons Water
Cream Cheese Frosting

Grease and flour 2 Easy Bake Oven pans.

Combine all ingredients and stir until well mixed.
Pour ½ of mix into each pan. Bake for 9 minutes each.

Remove from pan and allow to cool.

Apply Cream Cheese frosting between layers and
around cake.

9

Peanut Butter Cake

6 tablespoons Flour
4 teaspoons Sugar
¼ teaspoon Baking Powder
Dash Salt
6 teaspoons Milk
2 teaspoons Peanut Butter
frosting of choice

Combine flour, sugar, baking powder and salt in a bowl.

Add vanilla extract, milk and peanut butter and mix until smooth.

Pour batter into greased and floured Easy Bake Oven cake pan.

Bake each cake for 12 to 15 minutes or until side of cake separates from pan.

Remove cake and cool. Frost.

10

Angels White Cake Mix

1 cup Sugar
1½ cups Flour
1 teaspoon Baking Soda
½ teaspoon Salt
⅓ cup Shortening

In a medium bowl, combine sugar, flour, baking soda, and salt. Stir with a wire whisk until blended.

With a pastry blender, cut in shortening until mixture looks like fine breadcrumbs.

Spoon about ⅓ cup mixture into each of 10 small containers or ziploc bags.

Seal bags tightly and label with date and contents. Store in a cool dry place.

Use within 12 weeks. Makes 10 servings Cake Mix.

11

 # Angels White Cake

Mix 1 package of Angels White Cake Mix (page 11) with 1 tablespoon of water.

Stir well until smooth.

Bake in greased pan in oven until slightly brown

Birthday Cake

4 teaspoons Flour

2 teaspoons Cocoa Powder

1 tablespoon Sugar

⅛ teaspoon Baking Powder

1 dash Salt

⅛ teaspoon Vanilla

4 teaspoons Water

2 teaspoons Vegetable Oil

2 teaspoons frosting – your choice

Stir together: flour, cocoa, sugar, baking powder, salt, vanilla, water and oil.

Stir until batter is smooth and chocolate colored. Pour the batter into greased and floured cake pan.

Bake 13 – 15 minutes or until you see the sides of the cake separate from the pan.

Remove cake and cool. Makes 1 layer of cake.

Crazy Cake

4½ teaspoons Flour
3 teaspoons Sugar
¼ teaspoon Cocoa
⅛ teaspoon Baking Powder
Dash of Salt
⅛ teaspoon Vanilla
⅛ teaspoon Vinegar
1½ teaspoons Vegetable Oil

Mix together flour, sugar, cocoa, baking powder and salt.

Add vanilla, vinegar and vegetable oil.

Place into greased cake pan.

Pour 1 teaspoon water over batter.
Mix lightly with a fork but do not beat.

Bake for 10 minutes.

14

Raisin Spice Cake

¼ cup Sugar
½ tablespoon Shortening
Pinch ground Cinnamon
Pinch ground Nutmeg
Pinch of ground Allspice
Pinch Salt
¼ cup Raisins
⅓ cup Water
¼ teaspoon Baking Soda and ¼ teaspoon Baking Powder
½ cup all purpose Flour

Preheat oven.
In melting tray combine; sugar shortening, cinnamon, nutmeg, allspice, salt, raisins, and water. Melt for 10 minutes. Remove from heat and let cool.

Sift the flour, baking powder and baking soda all together. Add the flour mixture to the cooled raisin mixture. Stir just until combined.

Pour batter into prepared pan.
Bake for 10 minutes or until toothpick tests clean.

Kool Aid Cake Mix

1 cup Sugar
1½ cups Flour
1 teaspoon Baking Soda
½ teaspoon Salt
1 teaspoon Lemon Unsweetened Drink Powder -- (or any flavor Kool Aid)
⅓ cup Shortening

In a medium bowl, combine sugar, flour, baking soda, salt and drink powder. Stir with a wire whisk until blended.

With a pastry blender, cut in shortening until mixture looks like fine breadcrumbs.

Spoon about ⅓ cup of mix into each of 10 small containers or ziploc bags.

Seal bags tightly and label with date and contents.
Store in a cool dry place. Use within 12 weeks.
Makes 10 servings Cake Mix.

NOTES: Any flavor of Kool-Aid powder can be used for a wide variety of flavors.

16

Kool Aid Cake

1 package Kool Aid Cake Mix (page 16)
4 teaspoons water

Preheat play oven for 15 minutes.

Grease and flour a 4 inch miniature cake pan.

In a small bowl, combine cake mix and water.

Stir with a fork or spoon until blended and smooth.

Pour mixture into prepared pan.
Bake 12 to 13 minutes. Remove from oven.

Cool in pan on rack for 5 minutes.

Turn cake over onto a small plate. Remove pan.

Makes 2 small cakes.

Super Fun M and M's Cake

3 tablespoons instant chocolate cake mix (page 4)
1⅓ tablespoons water
M&M's Brand Milk Chocolate Mini's Bits

Preheat play oven 15 minutes.

Mix instant chocolate cake mix and water.

Pour mixture into greased cake pan.

Sprinkle M&M's bits over the top of the cake batter.

Bake 10-12 minutes.

Peach Upside Down Cake

¼ cup yellow Cake Mix (page 2)
3 teaspoons Peach Juice
2 slices Canned Peaches; drained
Brown Sugar

Grease pan lightly with butter.
Sprinkle brown sugar over bottom of pan.

Arrange thin slices of drained peaches over brown sugar.

Mash lightly with spoon.
Pour cake batter over peaches.

Bake about 20 minutes. Let cool.
Put cake on plate with peaches up.

NOTE: Vary by using canned pears, pineapple, apple or any favorite fruit.

Quick Cake

3 tablespoons purchased cake mix
(Duncan Hines, Betty Crocker, Jiffy)
1¼ teaspoons water

Preheat oven 15 minutes.

Blend cake mix and 1 tablespoon water – make sure not to add too much water. You want a traditional cake batter consistency.

Pour batter into greased and floured toy cake pan.

Bake 10-12 minutes.

# Princess Sparkle Tea Cakes

¼ cup All Purpose Flour
¼ teaspoon Baking Powder
⅛ teaspoon Salt
2 teaspoons Sugar
2 teaspoons Butter
4 teaspoons Milk
1 teaspoon multi-colored cookie decorations

Preheat play oven 15 minutes.

Mash together flour, baking powder, salt, sugar and butter until dough looks like medium-sized crumbs.

Slowly mix in the milk. Form dough into a loose ball and divide it into 4 pieces with a spoon.

Place a few dough pieces on greased sheet or pan. Sprinkle with cookie decorations over the top of the dough and push them in with your fingers.

Bake 20 minutes. Makes 4 tea cakes.

21

Baby Brownies

2½ tablespoons Sugar
1 teaspoon Vegetable Oil
⅛ teaspoon Vanilla
4 teaspoons Chocolate Syrup
2 teaspoons plus 1 tablespoon Flour

Sir together sugar, oil, vanilla, chocolate and flour until the batter is smooth and chocolate colored.

Pour batter into greased and floured pan.

Bake 15 minutes.

When cool, cut them into wedges or little squares.

Makes 6 wedges or ½ inch squares.

Chocolate Frosting Mix

2 cups Powdered Sugar, sifted
3 tablespoons Non Fat Dry Milk powder
½ cup Unsweetened Cocoa Powder
6 tablespoons Vegetable Shortening

In a medium bowl, combine icing sugar, milk powder and cocoa powder. (Sift cocoa if lumpy.)

With a pastry blender, cut in the shortening until mixture looks like fine breadcrumbs.

Spoon about ⅓ cup of mixture into each of 9 small containers or ziplock bags and seal tightly.

Label with date and contents.

Store in a cool dry place. Use within 12 weeks.

Makes 9 servings.

 # Chocolate Frosting

1 package Chocolate Frosting Mix (page 23)
¾ teaspoon water

In a small bowl, combine frosting mix and water.

Stir with a spoon until smooth.

Makes about ¼ cup.

Sparkly Frosting

4 teaspoons Vegetable Shortening
⅔ cup Powdered Sugar
¼ teaspoon Vanilla
2 teaspoons Milk
Colored sugar crystals for decoration

In a small bowl, mix together shortening, powdered sugar, vanilla and milk until smooth and creamy.

Spread 2 teaspoons of frosting on top of 1st layer.

Add 2nd layer and continue frosting.

Sprinkle with colored crystal sugars.

Frosts a 2 layer cake.

White Frosting Mix

2 cups Powdered Sugar, sifted
3 tablespoons Non Fat Dry Milk Powder
6 tablespoons Vegetable Shortening

In a medium bowl, combine powdered sugar and milk powder.

Stir with a wire whisk to blend.

With a pastry blender, cut in shortening until mixture looks like fine breadcrumbs.

Spoon about ⅓ cup mixture into each of 8 small containers or ziplock bags.

Seal bags tightly and label with date and contents.

Store in a cool dry place. Use within 12 weeks.

Makes 8 servings.

White Frosting

1 package White Frosting Mix (page 26)
¾ teaspoon water

In a small bowl, combine mix and water.

Stir well with a spoon until smooth and creamy.

Makes about ¼ cup frosting.

A drop or two of vanilla may be added if desired.

Cream Cheese Frosting Mix

1 cup Powdered (Icing) Sugar, sifted
4½ teaspoons instant nonfat Milk Powder
3 tablespoons Cream Cheese

Combine powdered sugar and milk powder, blend with wire whisk.

Cut in cream cheese with pastry blender or fork.

Spoon ⅓ cup mixture into each of 8 containers or ziploc bags.

Seal tightly and label with date and contents.

Store in refrigerator for up to 2 weeks.

Cream Cheese Frosting

1 package Cream Cheese Frosting Mix (page 28)
¾ teaspoon Water
Drop of Almond Extract

Combine mix, water and almond extract and stir well with spoon until smooth and creamy.

Makes ¼ cup

Peanut Butter Cream Frosting Mix

2 cups Powdered (Icing) Sugar, sifted
3 tablespoons non fat Powdered Milk
6 tablespoons Peanut Butter

In a medium bowl, combine powdered sugar and milk powder.

Stir with wire whisk to blend.

With a pastry blender, cut in peanut butter until mixture looks like fine breadcrumbs.

Spoon about ⅓ cup mixture into each 8 small containers or ziploc bags.

Seal tightly and label with date and contents.

Store in cool dry place. Use within 12 weeks.

30

Peanut Butter
Cream Frosting

1 package Peanut Butter Cream Frosting Mix (page30)
¾ teaspoon water

In a small bowl mix 1 package Peanut Butter Cream Frosting mix with water.

Stir well with a spoon until smooth and creamy.

Add a drop or two of vanilla if desired.

Each pack makes about ¼ cup of frosting.

Party Frosting

4 teaspoons Vegetable Shortening
⅔ cup Powdered Sugar
⅛ teaspoon Vanilla
2 teaspoons Milk
Colored sugar crystals for decoration

In a small bowl, mix together shortening, powdered sugar, vanilla and milk until smooth and creamy.

Spread frosting on top of cake and continue with sides.

Sprinkle with colored crystal sugars.

Frosts 2 cakes.

Angel Cookies

6 teaspoons Butter
3 teaspoons White Sugar
3 teaspoons Brown Sugar
pinch of Salt
¼ cup Flour
1/8 teaspoon Cream of Tartar
1/8 teaspoon Baking Soda

Cream together butter, sugars and salt.

Add flour, cream of tartar, and baking soda.

Bake 5 minutes.

Makes twelve one-inch cookies.

Thumbprint Cookies

1 tablespoon Powdered Sugar
2 tablespoons Butter
¼ teaspoon Vanilla
½ teaspoon Water
¼ cup Flour
Your favorite jelly

Stir together powdered sugar, butter, vanilla, water and flour until the flour disappears.

Roll the dough between your fingers and make 12 small balls, ½ inch each.

Place a few balls at a time on an un-greased sheet or pan with space between them.
Press your thumb into the middle of each ball to make a thumb print.

Bake 10 to 12 minutes, then remove.
Repeat until all the cookies are baked.

When the cookies are cool, fill each thumb print with jelly.
Makes 12 cookies.

Butter Cookies

6 teaspoons Butter
3 teaspoons Sugar
3 teaspoons Brown Sugar
¼ cup Flour
⅛ teaspoon Baking Powder
⅛ teaspoon Vanilla
1 pinch Salt

Preheat play oven for 15 minutes.
Spray Easy Bake pan with non-stick cooking spray.

Mix butter, sugars, and salt together. Add flour, baking powder, and vanilla. Stir to form batter.

½ teaspoon filled with dough will make one cookie.

Drop dough balls onto greased pan; allow room to spread.
Bake each batch 5-7 minutes. Let cool.

Makes 12 to 15 cookies.

Peanut Butter Cookies

¼ cup Flour
1½ tablespoons Peanut Butter
1 tablespoon Butter
2 teaspoons Sugar

In a bowl, mix together all ingredients to make a dough.

With your fingers roll into ½ inch balls.

Place 4 balls into the Easy Bake Oven pan and press down slightly with the tines of a fork.

Bake for 6 minutes. Cool.

Bake remaining balls 4 at a time.

Makes 12 cookies

Rice Krispie Treats

To make one treat:
1 teaspoon Butter
2 teaspoons Marshmallow Cream
Puffed Rice Cereal

Preheat oven for 15 minutes.
Place butter and marshmallow cream in the warming cup. Put on the warming tray and cover.

Warm for nine minutes stirring occasionally.

Half fill the other warming cup with puffed rice cereal. Thoroughly mix the puffed rice cereal with the warmed mixture of butter and marshmallow cream in a bowl.

Take a small amount from the bowl and form a cookie shape. Place the shapes on a plate.

Refrigerate for about ½ hour or until firm.

Cookie Mix

1½ cups quick cook Oats
¾ cup all purpose Flour
¼ teaspoon Baking Soda
¾ cup Brown Sugar, packed
½ cup Vegetable Shortening

In a medium bowl, combine oats, flour, baking soda and brown sugar. Stir to blend.

Cut in shortening with a pastry blender until mixture looks like fine breadcrumbs.

Spoon about ½ cup mixture into each of 8 small containers or ziplock bags. Seal bags tightly and label with date and contents. Store in a cool dry place.

Use within 12 weeks.

Makes 8 servings of Cookie Mix.

Each package makes 9 cookies.

Raisin
Chocolate Chip Cookies

1 package Cookie Mix (page 38)
2 teaspoons Water
1 tablespoon Raisins
1 tablespoon mini semi-sweet Chocolate Chips
Sugar for topping
Melted Butter

Preheat oven for 15 minutes.
In a small bowl, combine cookie mix, water, raisins and chocolate chips.

Stir with a spoon until mixture holds together in one big ball. Shape one teaspoon of dough at a time into a ball.

Arrange on an un-greased cookie sheet.

Butter bottom of a small drinking glass. Dip buttered glass bottom in sugar. Flatten each ball by pressing with sugar-coated glass. Bake 10 to 12 minutes.

Remove from oven and cool on a rack. Each package of mix makes about 9 cookies.

39

Chocolate Chip Cookies

1 teaspoon Sugar

1 tablespoon firmly packed Brown Sugar

2 teaspoons Butter

⅛ teaspoon Baking Powder

⅛ teaspoon Vanilla

1 teaspoon Water

3 tablespoons All purpose Flour

4 teaspoons semi-sweet Chocolate Chips

Stir together the sugars and margarine.
Add the baking powder, vanilla, water and flour,
stirring until flour disappears.

Mix in the chocolate chips.

Roll the dough between your fingers and make 12
small balls, 1 inch each.

Place a few balls in greased pan. Bake 10-12 minutes.

Repeat until all balls are done.

40

Choc Chip Peanut Cookies

¾ Cup Sifted All Purpose Flour
¾ teaspoon Milk
2 tablespoons Sugar
⅛ teaspoon Baking Soda
4 tablespoons Light Corn Syrup
Pinch Salt
2 tablespoons Shortening
¼ cup Peanut Butter
¼ cup semi-sweet Chocolate Chips

Preheat oven 15 minutes.
Combine flour, sugar, soda and salt.

Cut in shortening and peanut butter until mixture
resembles coarse meal. Blend in syrup and milk. Shape into
roll 2 inches in diameter; chill. Slice ⅛ to ¼ inch thick.

Place ½ the slices on un-greased cookie sheet; spread
each with ½ teaspoon peanut butter.
Sprinkle chocolate chips on top of peanut butter.

Cover with remaining cookie slices; seal edges with fork.

Bake for 12 minutes or until browned.

Layer Cookies

¼ cup Butter, melted
¼ cup Graham Cracker Crumbs
¼ cup flaked Coconut
3 tablespoons Chocolate Chips
3 tablespoons Butterscotch chips
¼ can sweetened Condensed Milk
¼ cup Nuts

Place butter in melting tray until completely melted. Transfer butter to cake pan.

Spread graham cracker crumbs over top.

Layer the coconut, then chocolate chips and the butterscotch chips.

Pour sweetened condensed milk over all. Top with nuts.

DO NOT MIX TOGETHER. Bake for 15 minutes.

Oreo Mud Pies

3 Oreo Cookies, separate + remove inner cream
2 tablespoons Butter
Scoop of Chocolate ice cream
Chocolate fudge sauce

Crush 4 halves of Oreo Cookies (choose your favorite method) until granular.

Place butter in melting tray until fully melted.

Transfer butter to cake pan.

Mix with crushed Oreo's and flatten to form a crust.

Bake in oven 10 minutes. Let crust cool completely.

Place scoop of ice cream and garnish with fudge sauce and remaining Oreo cookies broken into small pieces.

Butterscotch Chip Cookies

½ cup Sugar
¼ cup Shortening
¼ cup Sour Milk *See NOTE
¼ teaspoon Baking Soda
Dash Salt
Butterscotch Chips
NOTE Add ¼ teaspoon vinegar to milk to make sour milk*

Preheat oven 15 minutes.

Cream together sugar and shortening.

Add sour milk, soda and salt.

Stir in enough flour to make a stiff dough.
Divide dough in half and spread into greased cake pan.

Press Butterscotch chips into dough (in pattern if desired).
Bake for 10-12 minutes. Slice while still warm.

Cool before removing from pan.

Ginger Cookies

½ cup Sugar
½ cup Shortening
½ cup Dark Molasses
1 teaspoon Baking Soda
½ teaspoon Ground Ginger
½ teaspoon Cinnamon
2 cups All Purpose Flour

Preheat oven.

In a large bowl, cream together the sugar and shortening until smooth. Stir in molasses.

Combine the baking soda, ginger, cinnamon and 1¾ cups of the flour; blend into the molasses mixture.

Add more flour if necessary to make dough stiff enough to roll out.

Use remaining flour to dust rolling surface.

Roll dough out to ¼" thickness and cut with mini cookie cutters.   Bake for 7-10 minutes.

Santa's Cookies

½ cup Butter
½ cup Sugar
1 tablespoon Milk
½ teaspoon Vanilla
1¼ cups all purpose Flour
½ cup red candied Cherries, finely chopped
¼ cup Pecans, finely chopped
½ cup Coconut Flakes

Cream together butter and sugar until fluffy.
Add vanilla and milk, and mix well.
Add flour, cherries and pecans to form a stiff dough.

Place onto a lightly floured surface and form into an 8 inch log. Wrap in waxed paper and refrigerate 3 or more hours.

Grease and flour Easy-Bake Oven baking pans. Unwrap and slice dough into ¼ inch circles.

Place 2 cookies in each prepared pan and bake until beginning to brown around edges (about 20 minutes).

Cool pans on wire rack.

46

Oatmeal Fruit Bars

1 tablespoon Shortening or Butter
6 teaspoons Brown Sugar
¼ cup Flour
3 tablespoons Milk
⅛ teaspoon Baking Soda
2 tablespoons quick cook Rolled Oats
Dash Salt
2 teaspoons Applesauce or Marmalade

Mix shortening, sugar and salt.
Add flour, baking soda, oats and milk.

Mix well. Place ½ mixture in greased pan. Press down in pan with fingertips or back of spoon.

Spread with 2 teaspoons applesauce or marmalade.

Bake about 21 minutes. Let cool and cut into slices.

Use other half of mixture for second batch of bars

Gooey Caramel Layer Bars

2 tablespoons Butter
⅓ cup Graham Cracker Crumbs
2 tablespoons semisweet Chocolate Chips
2 tablespoons Butterscotch Chips
2 tablespoons flaked Coconut
2 tablespoons sweetened Condensed Milk
2 tablespoons chopped Walnuts

Melt butter in Easy-Bake Oven baking pan.

Sprinkle graham cracker crumbs evenly over butter.
Sprinkle on the chocolate and butterscotch chips.

Sprinkle on a layer of flaked coconut and top with walnuts.

Pour condensed milk evenly over everything.

Bake for about 15 minutes. Allow to cool.

Honey Bunches Snack

Makes 2

Cooking Spray

¼ cup Honey Bunches of Oats cereal

¼ cup Life Cereal

1 tablespoon Honey

1 tablespoon Peanuts

Preheat oven for about 10 minutes.

Spray 2 Easy Bake Oven pans with cooking spray.

Mix the cereals together.

Pour honey over the top and mix.

Spoon half of each mixture into the two pans.

Sprinkle with peanuts.

Put one pan in the oven at a time and bake for
5 minutes or until it smells done.

Blueberry Danish

¼ cup Commercial Biscuit Mix
½ tablespoon Butter
¾ teaspoon Sugar
4 teaspoons Milk
½ tablespoon Blueberry Pie Filling

Combine biscuit mix, butter and sugar. Mix until crumbly.
Add milk, stir well until soft dough forms.

Place ½ teaspoonfuls onto lightly greased baking pan.
Make indentation in each by pressing thumb into middle.
Fill indent with blueberry pie filling.
Bake until golden brown.

To make glaze:
¼ cup Powdered Sugar
1 teaspoon Water
2 drops Vanilla.
Mix ingredients together until smooth.
Drizzle glaze over top.

Note: Vary by using different pie fillings.

Breakfast Biscuits

¼ cup Commercial Biscuit Mix
4 teaspoons Milk

Combine biscuit mix and milk with a fork.

Drop half-teaspoonfuls onto a well greased pan.

Bake 10 minutes.

Scones

1 tablespoon Sour Cream
⅛ teaspoon Baking Soda
⅓ cup all purpose Flour
1 tablespoon Sugar
⅛ teaspoon Baking Powder
⅛ teaspoon Cream of Tartar
⅛ teaspoon Salt
1 tablespoon Butter
1 tablespoon Raisins; optional

Grease and flour Easy-Bake Oven pan.
Blend sour cream and baking soda in a small bowl and set aside.

Mix together flour, sugar, baking powder, cream of tartar and salt. Cut in butter with a pastry blender.

Stir in sour cream mixture until just moistened and mix in raisins if using. Knead dough just a little on lightly floured surface. Do not over-knead or the scones will be hard.

Roll or pat dough into ½ inch thick round. Cut into wedges and place on prepared baking sheet.

Bake for 15 minutes.

52

Peanut Butter Fudge

1 cup Powdered Sugar
5 teaspoons Milk
1 teaspoon Butter
½ teaspoon Vanilla
4 teaspoons Cocoa Powder
6 teaspoons smooth Peanut Butter

Mix sugar, milk, butter, vanilla and cocoa until smooth.

Grease two baking pans with butter. Spoon mix into pans about ¼" deep. Spread 3 teaspoons peanut butter over mix.

Spoon another layer of mix ¼" thick over peanut butter.

Bake each pan about 5 minutes. Let cool. (For quicker cooling, place in refrigerator 5 minutes)

Makes about 5 servings.

Snow Mounds

6 teaspoons Shortening, or soft Butter
3 teaspoons Powdered Sugar
⅛ teaspoon Vanilla
¼ cup Flour
Dash of Salt
2 tablespoons finely chopped Walnuts
Powdered Sugar for rolling

Cream together butter and 3 teaspoons powdered sugar. Blend in vanilla, flour and salt.

Add walnuts and mix well.

Shape into 1 inch balls. Place 3 balls onto well greased pan. Flatten slightly. Bake 5 minutes.

When cool, roll in powdered sugar.

Repeat until all the mounds are cooked.

Makes 10 to 12.

Haystacks

⅔ cup Butterscotch Chips
1 cup Chow Mein Noodles
⅓ cup Spanish Peanuts

Melt chips over melting tray.

Remove from heat.

Stir in chow mein noodles and peanuts.

Drop by tablespoonful onto wax paper to let harden.

(You can also use chocolate or caramel chips)

Butterscotch Candy

¼ cup Butterscotch morsels
2 teaspoons Butter
Candy Molds

Put butter and morsels into the melting pan and place the pan on the Warm/Melt area top of the oven.

Heat for 15 minutes. (You can also do this in the microwave stirring every 30 seconds)

Stir gently every 5 minutes.

Using a spoon, fill the candy molds with melted butterscotch.

Place the molds in the refrigerator for 30 minutes or until firm. Remove from molds.

Makes about 6 candies, depending on the mold size.

Baked Apple

1 large Apple
Butter for greasing pan
Cinnamon
½ teaspoon sugar

Wash apple. Slice across apple to make rings ½" thick.

Use center slices. Remove center core.

Grease pan with butter. Place one apple ring in pan.

Sprinkle lightly with cinnamon, then with ½ teaspoon sugar.

Dot top with ¼ teaspoon butter.

Bake about 20 minutes.

Raisin Bread Pudding

1 egg
½ cup Milk
¼ teaspoon Vanilla
4 tablespoons Sugar
4 slices Raisin Bread

Topping:
Cinnamon
1 teaspoon milk
¼ teaspoon Butter

Break bread into small pieces.Mix all ingredients together in a bowl.

Grease 3 pans lightly with butter. Fill pans ½ full and press down. Sprinkle tops lightly with cinnamon.

Add 1 teaspoon milk and ¼ teaspoon butter on top of each pudding.

Bake for 20 to 25 minutes.

Twisty Cheese Straws

8 ounce can Pillsbury Crescent Rolls
2 teaspoons Butter; melted
½ cup cheese; grated
Garlic Salt

Divide dough in half and form into 2 rectangles. Press perforations to seal.

Brush one rectangle with butter, then sprinkle with cheese and garlic salt.

Place second rectangle of dough over the top.

Cut into ½ inch strips. Twist each strip five times.

Pinch the ends to seal.

Place on an un-greased pan and bake until golden brown.

Home Made Bisquick Mix

8 cups Flour
4 tablespoons Sugar
4 tablespoons Baking Powder
4 teaspoons Salt
1 cup Shortening

Mix together flour, baking powder, salt and sugar in a large bowl, blending well.

Cut in the shortening with a pastry blender until the mixture resembles fine breadcrumbs.

Store in airtight container until needed.

Makes about 10½ cups.

Cheese Biscuits

½ cup Bisquick Mix (see previous recipe)
2 tablespoons plus 2 teaspoons Milk
2 tablespoons shredded Cheddar Cheese
1 tablespoon Parmesan Cheese

Topping:
1 tablespoon Butter
⅛ teaspoon Garlic Powder
¼ teaspoon dried Parsley

Stir together baking mix, milk and cheeses until soft dough forms.

Drop spoonfuls onto un-greased pan.

Bake for 15 minutes or until bottoms are lightly browned.

Melt butter in warming tray, stir in garlic powder and parsley flakes. Brush over warm biscuits.

Cheesy Quesadilla

Makes 1

1 Tortilla
Shredded Cheese

Cut a small flour tortilla into wedges small enough to fit the pan.

Sandwich shredded cheese between two wedges and bake for 4-6 minutes or until cheese melts

Pizza

2 tablespoons all purpose Flour
⅛ teaspoon Baking powder
1 dash Salt
1 teaspoon Butter
2¼ teaspoons Milk
1 tablespoon Pizza Sauce
1½ tablespoons Shredded Mozzarella Cheese

Stir together flour, baking powder, salt and butter until dough looks like medium-sized crumbs.

Slowly add milk while stirring.

Shape dough into a ball and place in a greased pan. Use your fingers to pat the dough evenly over the bottom of the pan, then up the sides.

Pour the pizza sauce evenly over the dough, then sprinkle with the cheese. Bake 20 minutes.

Makes 1 pizza.

Cheese Omelette

1 Egg
4 teaspoons shredded Cheddar Cheese
1 pinch Salt
1 pinch Pepper
Cooking Spray

Preheat the oven for 15 minutes.

Spray 2 Easy Bake Oven pans with cooking spray.

Whisk the egg in a bowl using a fork.

Divide the egg between 2 pans.

Sprinkle with salt and pepper.

Sprinkle 2 teaspoons of cheese on top of each egg.

Bake for 15 minutes.

I hope you enjoyed this book and cooking lots of delicous treats.

66